THE VOCALIST'S TOOLBOX

A Portable Workshop for Singers

Vivian Dettbarn-Slaughter, D.S.M.

Cover art, *Leaf Opals,* by Michael Slaughter.

To all my students, past and present

CONTENTS

ACKNOWLEDGMENTS

This project would not have been possible without the support and encouragement of my family and students. Many thanks to several people for reading the manuscript and giving their input: Michael Allen, Professor of Theatre at Adrian College; Sandra Agans-Krueger of the Agans-Krueger Voice Studio; Rod Robles, Voice Class Instructor for Santa Barbara City College Continuing Education; and Dr. Stanley Workman, Voice Instructor and Director of Choral Activities at Shawnee State University.

I want to thank my son, Ryan Dettbarn, for all of the interesting conversations we have had about life and music. Our talks have always helped me to see through the eyes of a student.

I especially wish to thank my husband, Michael Slaughter, for his loving support throughout this process. I am grateful for his insightful comments, his willingness to listen as I worked out ideas, his point of view as a teacher, and his editing of the book. Thanks also to Michael for his beautiful cover photo, *Leaf Opals.*

Singing is a skill, as much as an art.

1

WHAT ARE YOUR GOALS?

A wise teacher once told me that whenever I received an assignment, I should ask myself what I wanted to learn, rather than waiting to see what I found. I tell my students to go into their practice sessions knowing what they would like to hear, rather than waiting to see what "comes out." With that in mind, I suggest beginning with this question: *In order to be a good performer, what are the skills, strategies and tools I need to have?* Rather than just saying *I want to be a great singer,* you will be much more successful if you are clear and specific. Consider these goals:

- ✓ I want to be able to sing more easily.
- ✓ I want to be able to sing without running out of breath.
- ✓ I want to improve my tone and range.
- ✓ I want to sing in many languages without difficulty.
- ✓ I want to be a better sight-reader.
- ✓ I want to be less nervous when I perform.
- ✓ I want to know how to make a full sound without pushing.

When you go on a quest for treasure, you should probably know exactly what you're looking for. The job will be simpler, and the path to your goal will be easier to find.

SINGER'S TOOL:
KNOW YOUR GOALS

THINK ABOUT WHAT YOU WANT

- What are some of the improvements you would like to see?

- What are two or three of your long-range singing goals?

- Are there specific ways to achieve the goals you have in mind?

2

WHAT ARE THE TOOLS?

My job is to help students who are discovering and refining their talents. When I teach a lesson, work with a choir, or present a workshop, I bring my mental toolbox of teaching techniques and experience. I unpack the tools and use each one until the student is able to sing more easily and beautifully. With this repertoire of techniques and suggestions, I have been able to help many voice students, actors, choral singers and teachers. Once you have begun using these singing tools, you will notice improvements in your phrasing, tone, support, sight reading, *legato* technique, and breath management.

The book includes planning strategies, study tools, and a practice guide to help you to make the best use your time. If you can make time, you can make improvements.

The section about learning music will be helpful when tackling new assignments. Many singers start by immediately singing through a song, but they soon find that trying to learn the notes, rhythms, phrasing, and diction all at once is like juggling. Experienced singers know that the best plan is to simplify things and learn each element separately. After using the tools in the book, you will find that when the piece is "reassembled," all the complexities of the music will be woven together, and every strand will be under control.

There are special issues facing actors and choral singers, since finding the time to work on music outside of rehearsal can be challenging. Using *The Vocalist's Toolbox* and the companion CD will optimize your practice time so you can work more efficiently. It has become part of a routine for many of my students as they prepare for auditions and performances.

I have included a basic chart of the International Phonetic Alphabet (IPA), which will help you as you learn how to sing in different languages. By learning the symbols, the words can be written in a system of *sounds* that work in any language.

The vocalise exercises in the second half of the book are written in treble and bass clef. You may choose to read the music in the clef that is most familiar to you, or familiarize yourself with the alternate clef. Each vocalise is shown once, but the companion CD accompaniments include two complete cycles of repetitions for high and low voices. All of the exercises are suitable for any beginning or intermediate singer, and advanced students may wish to sing them in a more extended range.

A short section about *solfège* will introduce the traditional sight-singing system, and each vocalise in the book includes a *solfège* option. This book uses the *moveable do* system with no accidentals. Further information about *moveable do* and the *solfège* system can be researched in books, or online.

Most singers need individual support as they work on their vocal skills, and they need a simple daily routine. After many years of teaching, I have found that these tools and techniques result in consistent success.

3

BODY AND BREATH

Before you begin, look in a mirror and observe the way you are standing. When people hear the words *stand up straight,* they try to "stand at attention" by pulling *up* the rib cage, pressing *up* from the middle of the back, pulling *up* the shoulders and tightening the muscles around the hips. When we were kids, my sister and I would have breath-holding contests, and we would pull our shoulders *up* and pull our abdominal muscles *in* as we each tried to win. In lessons I have seen many beginning students using this same painful, tense posture to take a breath or indicate readiness. This is the *opposite* of a good singing stance. Your shoulders should be in the same position as when you lie on your back, and you should allow the breath to create abdominal expansion.

It's also important to stand with your weight over the arches of your feet. Close your eyes and stand quietly. Notice if you have a tendency to roll forward toward your toes, or backward toward your heels. Settling yourself over your arches can give you a pleasant, weightless sensation, and clears away some tension. What you are feeling is a sense of ease and flexibility in your back, your neck, and your joints, which can make a noticeable improvement in the sound.

A balanced stance and flexible breath support will help you to feel more energized. It will also give you a sense of ease. Doing a few breath exercises at the start of a practice session can be helpful, and will prepare you to focus on the work.

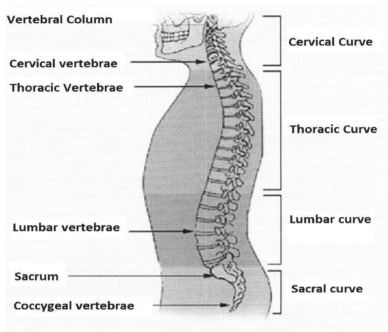

This illustration shows the natural curve of the spine. Proper alignment and posture allows the curve to remain intact, rather than trying to "straighten up", pushing the rib cage up and forward.

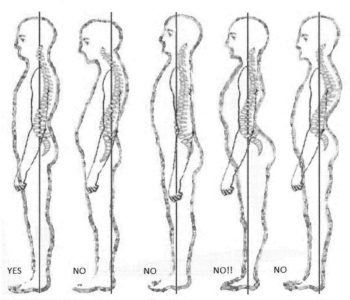

The figure in the middle is pressing the spine out of natural alignment. The figure on the **far left** is standing correctly. The others are creating stress and tension, with the weight pulling them too far forward or backward.

HISS AND SIZZLE

Get a timer and get ready to analyze your breath capacity. Think about maintaining an imaginary open space between your hips and the lower ribs, and a big airy space at the base of your skull. Hiss gently on an "s" sound for as long as possible, standing tall and maintaining a balanced singing posture. Follow this by singing a "z" sound for as long as possible, continuing to stand in a balanced and easy posture with your weight over your arches. Using the timer during the exercises will help you to extend the duration of your breath every time you practice. These exercises show how efficiently you use your breath.

BREATHE IN THE SHAPE OF A SQUARE

This is called a "square" breath, because there are four steps.

INHALE	HOLD	EXHALE	HOLD
1 2 3 4	1 2 3 4	1 2 3 4	1 2 3 4

You may find that you inhale too quickly, or maybe you don't completely exhale at first. With practice, your breathing will flow at an easy, predictable rate. Challenge yourself, and gradually work up to eight beats. With practice, you can use this exercise to settle yourself when you are getting ready to perform.

BE CAREFUL

When you hold your breath, be sure to
release tension in your throat, jaw, back and shoulders.

THE UPSIDE-DOWN-RIGHT-SIDE-UP BREATH

Starting with arms stretched up toward the ceiling, INHALE for a count of eight beats while lowering your arms all the way down to your sides.

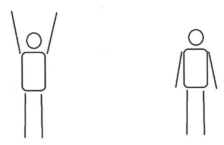

Next, EXHALE for a count of eight beats while slowly lifting your arms out to the side and up toward the ceiling again. Do this several times.

While this exercise may seem confusing at first, it will help you to be aware of the tendency to collapse your body during exhalation. It will also encourage you NOT to *push up and out* during inhalation.

NEVER INHALE OR EXHALE TO
THE POINT OF TENSION OR STRAIN.

SINGER'S TOOL: POSTURE AND BREATH EXERCISES

- Look in the mirror and observe the way you are standing.

- Close your eyes and check your balance. Is your weight falling forward or backward? Put your weight over the arches of your feet.

- Hiss gently on an "s" sound for as long as possible.

- Hiss gently on a "z" sound for as long as possible.

- Practice the Upside-Down Right-Side-Up breath.

- Practice the Square Breath.

INHALE	HOLD	EXHALE	HOLD
1 2 3 4	1 2 3 4	1 2 3 4	1 2 3 4

QUESTIONS

Were the hiss and sizzle timings similar? Make this a goal.

Did you breathe in and out evenly on the Square Breath?

How is your stance?

MUSIC

BREATH

VOWELS

CONSONANTS

VOICE

DICTION

RHYTHM

SING

VOCAL PRACTICE BEAUTIFUL

MELODY

4

MAKING THE SOUND

The vocal exercises in this book use the "pure" vowels of Italian, Latin and Spanish. English words contain many combinations of these "pure" vowels, as well as short, more difficult vowel sounds. For example, try holding the vowel in the words *it*, *love* and *cat* for four beats. These "short" English vowels are difficult to extend. You may notice that open vowels in words like *far* or *be* are easier to hold. The crossover sound between the English and Italian sounds is the vowel "e," as in the word *let*.

Here are the five basic vowel sounds. Later on you will find an introduction to the nuts and bolts of sound symbols, the International Phonetic Alphabet (IPA).

> ➢ a   as in *father*

> ➢ e   as in *feather*

> ➢ i   sounds like the double vowel in *see*

> ➢ o   without closing the mouth to finish the sound

> ➢ u   as in *rule*

INCORPORATING THE CONSONANTS

Many enthusiastic students tend to clench their jaws and spit the consonants at first, believing that they are pronouncing clearly. This kind of effort actually results in poor pronunciation, and lots of tension. You will have a much better result if you use the consonants as connections and bridges, not hurdles. Consonant/vowel combinations are the link between practice and performance, so I suggest practicing on single syllables to improve your diction. You will find that the consonants are actually part of the process of exhalation. Breath should always be moving through *every* letter of *every* syllable you sing.

HUMMING AND DRINKING STRAWS

Lip trills, the "oo" sound sung through straws, and humming exercises are known as *semi-occluded vocal tract phonation* techniques. By buzzing on lip trills, humming on *m, n,* or *ng,* and singing through straws, the air pressure in the vocal tract is equalized and balanced above and below the vocal folds. The result is a more efficient use of the breath, which in turn creates more resonance and makes singing easier. Each of the vocalises in the book has a list of different ways to sing the repetitions, including the semi-occluded phonation techniques. By trying all of the options, you can customize and vary your vocal routine.

The lip trill *sounds* similar to a rolled "r." Blow air on a "boo" sound through loosely closed lips, with the back teeth apart and the tip of the tongue behind the lower front teeth. Use enough pressure to make the lips buzz. If this is difficult at first, press your fingers into the sides of your cheeks, matching your fingertips with the line of your back teeth. If you're using enough breath, this will eventually result in a great lip trill.

The "m" hum is best done with lips barely closed. Don't bite down on your lips, and keep your back teeth apart. The "n" hum places the tip of your tongue behind your front upper teeth.

The "ng" hum can be set up by saying "king." Sustain the "ng," and put the tip of your tongue behind your lower front teeth. For the "n" and "ng" you should have your mouth <u>open</u>.

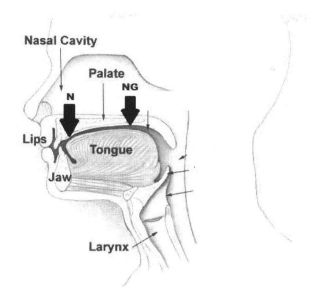

Singing through a drinking straw may seem like a strange idea, but the process can make an immediate and surprising improvement in the sound. **Blow through** the straw. **Don't hum** through it. There shouldn't be any air escaping around the straw. The sound will be quiet, but you will notice the intensity and steadiness of the way you are using your breath.

This feeling is called support, which is a steady, coordinated use of your body and breath. The words and notes change constantly, but support is the unifying element that makes everything work.

Once you have mastered the basic straw technique, sing a melody through a small (1/16th-inch diameter) straw. Using the smaller straw gives a strong sensation of steady breath support. Be sure you are using a small straw, not a divided coffee stirrer.

After "playing" the small straw a few times, sing normally, and you will hear and feel an immediate change in resonance and clarity. Be sure you release tension in your neck when you work this way, and use a new straw every time you practice!

Your singing depends on the skillful balance of consonants, vowels, and breath. You will soon discover that these elements work together in a continuous cycle.

- Practice the lip trill: blowing air on a "*boo*" sound to make the lips buzz. Keep the back teeth apart. Press your fingers into the sides of your cheeks, and match your fingertips with the line of your back teeth. This one takes practice!

- Hum on an "ng" sound, sliding up and down over the interval of a fourth or fifth, making pitch glides, or "hills:"

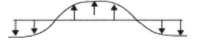

- Now make the hills while blowing through a small straw.

- Play your hills for a few minutes, with a relaxed throat.

- Sing a few "lip trill hills."

- Try the techniques with the vocalises in this book.

QUESTIONS

Do you consider vocalizing to be a tool to "warm up," a technique-building process, or both?

Have you tried using part of a song as a vocal exercise?

5

HEALTH AND PERFORMANCE

There are special issues for singers who haven't established a regular routine. Practicing your music on your own can be very challenging, and regular rehearsals already take up a lot of your creative time. It is common for people to feel the pressure of the time crunch during the weeks before a performance, but regular practice and rest are part of the formula for success. You can sing well while keeping a full work or class schedule, but not if you avoid sleep, eat fast food, and drink too much caffeine.

Maintain good health, because *you should not sing if you're sick.* If you must be at a rehearsal, be sure that you don't pose a health risk to the group. Ask your director for permission to take notes, follow all directions, and *mouth* the words silently. Whispering or singing "lightly" can do a lot of damage to your voice when you're ill. Save your voice for the next rehearsal.

Voice teachers and music directors seem to give the same health and practice advice, whether they are preparing students for a choral performance, a service, a recital, an audition, a musical or an opera. Good health is the result of good habits.

SINGER'S TOOL:
GOOD HEALTH HABITS

- Stay away from people who are ill.

- Rest, even when you think you can power through!

- Aim for a balanced nutrition and exercise plan. Choose your food for nutritional benefit, not for convenience.

- Hydrate, hydrate, hydrate. Drinking enough water is the best way to stay well. Health professionals say you should drink half your body's weight *in ounces* every day.

- Avoid the caffeine. It's a diuretic, and if you're not hydrated, your body won't be able to work properly.

- Wash your hands often, and use hand sanitizer when you are around people during cold and flu season.

- If you don't feel well enough to exercise or sing, take that cue from your body and take a break.

QUESTIONS

What do you do to maintain good health?

Are you *proactive* about staying well, or do you have to resort to being *reactive* when you become tired or ill?

6

CHORAL SINGERS: HIDDEN IN PLAIN SIGHT

Gasp, hold, sing as loud as you can, and... BLEND! This is not what the director wants, but many earnest and dedicated singers get caught up in the moment during their ensemble rehearsals and sing *fortissimo* whenever possible. If you sing in a choir, or in the chorus of a staged production, you may not always pay attention to what you are doing *to* or *with* your unique voice.

You are hidden in plain sight in the middle of a group, and when everyone is singing, it's very hard to know exactly how you sound. Singing loudly to hear yourself over everyone else will cause you to push, and it is possible to permanently injure your voice. Being swept away in the experience is half the fun, but don't forget to use common sense to protect your voice.

Most directors are experienced singers who are concerned about vocal technique, but in an ensemble rehearsal they are addressing the issues of the group. Your daily routine will get your singing voice in shape, and your conductor will be happy to have a chorus filled with smart singers who know how to avoid straining and injuring their voices.

✓ Warm up before rehearsals. Choral exercises are designed to get everyone working together with a great ensemble sound, but group exercises don't address individual needs.

✓ Practice your music on your own, and you will know what it feels like to sing in a healthy way. If you want to make an important contribution, practice your part.

✓ The conductor is showing you *when* to breathe, but you should know *how* to breathe. If you wait until the entrance cue to breathe, you might gasp and then sing with tension. Watch the director, but plan ahead.

✓ Blending. This is one of the goals of beautiful ensemble singing. A well-blended choral sound is like a great orchestra, with the members of each section performing with matched tone colors. Your job is to be careful that you're not holding your breath or creating tension in your body, while trying to make the tone colors that your director wants.

✓ Remember: individual practice will help you to develop techniques for singing and breathing correctly, even while surrounded by other singers. Take care of your voice. Don't lose yourself in the crowd.

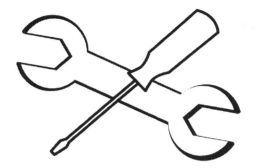

SINGER'S TOOL: care for your choral voice

- Practice your choral music in the same way you would practice a solo.

- If you learn your part carefully, you won't need to listen to the singers around you to find the notes.

- Don't increase your volume to be able to hear yourself over everyone else. Rely on the work you have done in your practice, and you won't push your voice in rehearsal.

- Maintain good health!!

QUESTIONS

Are you aware of the importance of your unique contribution to the choir? Each singer is vital in any choral ensemble.

Have you practiced the things that your director has emphasized? If the director asks you to bring a pencil to rehearsal, work on the sections that have been marked.

A famous musician was approached in New York City by someone who seemed to be lost.

The person asked, "How do you get to Carnegie Hall?"

The musician replied: "Practice, practice, practice."

7

YOUR DAILY PRACTICE SESSION

"What should I do? How long should I practice? How is practice different from singing through the music?"

Practicing is an adventure in experimentation, curiosity and self-awareness. It challenges you on many levels, including musicianship, imagination, and organizational skills. You are cross-training in the arts by studying poetic texts in different languages, working with teachers, accompanists and conductors, and improving your performance skills. You should practice your artistic *and* practical skills every day.

- ✓ Sing in a room without distractions. It isn't possible to practice while doing homework, watching TV, listening to other music, chatting or texting. Focus is important.

- ✓ Stand when you practice. Sitting at the piano while you sing, or "practicing" while driving are bad ideas. Stand the way you would in a performance, and tap into your enthusiasm, energy and skills.

- ✓ Use a mirror. Be brave and creative. That face in the mirror is your *student,* not yourself.

✓ Bring a journal, and make notes if you have questions or insights. Refer to your notes at every session, and bring the notes to your lessons. Celebrate your successes, don't just criticize yourself. I often ask students to compliment their work, but most can't think of anything good to say. You deserve recognition when you make progress.

✓ When you sing with a sound file, use external speakers. Headphones don't allow you to hear yourself accurately.

✓ Use a metronome. You can find metronomes in a wide range of prices, or use them free online or on your phone.

✓ Bring a pencil, and always have water.

✓ Start your session with breathing exercises to create a calm atmosphere. If you enjoy yoga, *tai chi*, dance, or stretches for sports, you may find that these disciplines will help you prepare for your singing practice.

✓ Warm up with five or ten minutes of vocalizing. The way you prepare is extremely important, because the exercises affect your ability to sing the music you want to perform.

✓ If the goal of your practice session is to work on technical improvement, continue with the exercises. Singing a complete set of the vocalises with the accompaniment CD will give you about thirty minutes of sustained practice.

✓ If the goal of your practice session is to work on music, practice for about 20 minutes after you vocalize, and then take a break. Try singing at different times during the day to find out what works best for you.

✓ Singing for more than 30 minutes can be tiring. Don't sing for hours, no matter how much you love the music, and don't sing when you're sick. Never push yourself to fatigue or exhaustion. *Singing is a physical skill.* Overuse of the singing muscles with an inflamed throat or vocal cords can lead to strain and permanent damage.

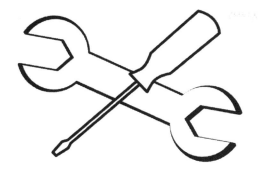

SINGer'S TOOL:
YOUR DaILY PraCTICE

- Schedule a practice time, and work in a place where you can concentrate. Work on your skills every day.

- Make a plan for your session, so you can set a goal and achieve it. In addition to singing your music, you want to target things to improve.

- Keep a journal to remind yourself about questions and improvements you have noticed. You'll be surprised at what you can accomplish when you monitor your own progress.

QUESTIONS

Have you noticed that you have an individual practicing style? You might be someone who does well in short sessions with lots of breaks, or you might be better at concentrating on a specific skill for 20 minutes before doing something else.

Do you give yourself good feedback, or are you extremely critical of yourself? Being honest with yourself also means you can celebrate your success. Feeling good about your work will remove tension, which will also improve your practice.

interpretation

rhythm text easy

support melody

Plan

Learn

poetry everything melodies

skill

sing strategies practice

diction Prepare

research art language plan

learn idea

sections

breath Pronounce listen

steps

Translate accompaniment composer

words singing understand

performing work music

8

STEPS TO LEARNING MUSIC

"I listen to the music, and then I sing it. After going over it several times, I know it. I might not have all the right rhythms at first, and maybe I don't know all the pronunciations yet, but that comes later. I don't know what it sounds like with the piano, but I'll learn my part and skip the rests until I have an accompanist. After that, it will all come together."

What this singer doesn't realize is that un-learning will take at least twice as long as getting it right the first time. Here's a list of easy, logical steps. The process is actually quick, enjoyable, and rewarding. Avoiding mistakes in the beginning will save time later on.

- ✓ **Make a chart:** Divide the piece into small sections, and name each one. Identify the sections that you know you can learn easily, and work with a teacher on strategies for learning the more complex parts.

- ✓ **Translate words** if they are in an unfamiliar language, and **learn the pronunciation**. Write them in International Phonetic Alphapet (IPA.)

- ✓ **Understand the words** of the text. Even if the piece is in English, you need to understand the full meaning of the poetry. This is especially important if the piece is from a show, opera, choral work, or a larger group of songs. Understanding the general idea is a good start, but it will be more interesting to learn the whole story.

✓ **Pronounce the words** until the diction flows easily.

✓ **Practice the text aloud**, using singing volume and breath support. Speak with support to make a "bridge" to singing.

✓ **Tap the rhythm** of the melody several times, and include the rests!

✓ **Tap the rhythm as you listen to the accompaniment**. You need to understand how everything fits together.

✓ **Speak the rhythm** on a syllable like *ta,* and then speak the rhythm as you listen to the accompaniment.

✓ **Sing the melody on** a syllable like *la* to learn the pitches.

✓ **Sing the music with the accompaniment.**

Voilà! The music is yours.

Once you have learned the music, do some research to find out more about the composer and the poet. Add this to the work you've done on the text, and your interpretation will be more meaningful and interesting, both for you and for your audience.

After you have learned and memorized a piece, don't stop looking at the music. It's very easy to start inventing new melodies or words if you don't keep the music nearby. You might be practicing mistakes that will be hard to change later.

Practice as if you are performing. If you sing without volume or support, or speed through the parts you know best and skip the tough stuff, your practice won't be reliable. Prepare like a star athlete, and you will be able to play the game. Make it easy by working through the steps.

Remember, *singing is a skill, as much as an art*.

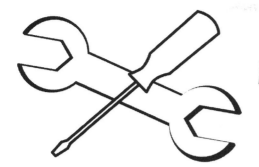

SINGER'S TOOL:
LEARNING A PIECE OF MUSIC

Follow the steps in this order:

1. Make a chart and identify the major sections.

2. Translate the words and learn the pronunciation.

3. Understand the meaning of the text.

4. Practice reading the text aloud.

5. Tap the rhythm of the melody, including the rests.

6. Tap the rhythm as you listen to the accompaniment.

7. Speak the rhythm on *ta.*

8. Speak the rhythm as you listen to the accompaniment.

9. Sing the melody on a syllable like *la* to learn the pitches.

10. Sing the music with the accompaniment.

creativity

ability

confidence

practice

imagination

focus

9

THE PRACTICE GAME

After learning a new piece of music, most people practice by starting at the beginning and working until they get to the end. This seems logical, but once you have applied all of the steps in the previous chapter, you should try practicing it backward. I like this method because it addresses several potential issues:

- You may be learning by ear, instead of reading the music.

- If you always start at the beginning, you might practice the early measures of the piece twenty times more than the last measures. This explains the terror that creeps in as you near the end of a new piece. Terror = tension.

- You will learn more about the phrases if you decide to think in both directions. Be flexible about your approach.

Once you have completed the basic steps in the previous chapter, try the practice game. It seems odd, but it is extremely efficient, and you will know the music *very* well.

SINGER'S TOOL:
THE PRACTICE GAME

- Learn the last few notes. Sing with confidence. Music seems achievable once you know where you're going.

- Sing the last few measures, leading up to the final notes.

- Back up a few notes or measures, and go to the end.

- Go to an earlier section, and start the process again.

- Learn small sections this way until you get back to the beginning. This works well on difficult passages. If you start by going backward, it will feel like less of a challenge.

Here is an example. Say it aloud:
Once upon a time there were three bears.

Bears. Three bears. Were three bears. There were three bears. Time there were three bears. A time there were three bears. Upon a time there were three bears. Once upon a time there were three bears. You get the idea.

This can be applied to notes, measures, phrases, or small sections of a piece. It can also be applied to the syllables of text in a language that might be difficult for you. Everything can be broken down into easy, small sections.

With the backward technique, you're involved with the game, and it doesn't feel like a big project. It will feel like a *process.* The reward will be obvious when you finally sing your music again from the beginning. It will feel as though you are sailing into familiar territory, instead of heading into uncharted waters.

10

BE PATIENT

You are surrounded by sound files, the Internet, radio, concerts, videos and so forth. You have a well-defined sense of what you like because you are an involved, sophisticated listener and music consumer.

With your extensive listening experience, you probably know exactly what you want to hear when you sing. But what if you're not hearing it yet? It can be frustrating when you don't make the progress you want, but you need to be realistic about the time it takes to hear a change in your singing.

Is it possible to read a book about skiing and then head down the mountain? Should you read an article about deep-sea diving and jump into the ocean, expecting to excel?

Your high expectations are important, and they will help you achieve your goals if you balance them with active skill-building. Smart practice, in addition good work in rehearsals and lessons, will reward you with progress.

Be thoughtful, expect good things, and remember that a skill takes time to master. Learn in depth, and you will be on your way to achieving what you really want.

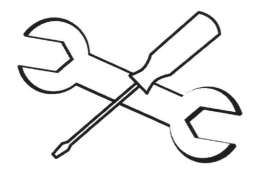

SINGER'S TOOL: Track Your Progress

| Start | Spectrum of Skill-Building Progress | Finish |

You will always be somewhere on this chart as you build your singing skills. Rather than being completely right or completely wrong, you are making progress!

- Make a checklist of tasks to complete when you're learning a piece. There are lots of small steps in the process, so keep track of the things you have accomplished.

- Give yourself credit for the successes along the way.

QUESTIONS

Are you goal-oriented?
Are you process-oriented?
Have you decided to balance the two in order to make progress?
If so, you will have an easier time learning any skill.

11

SOLFÈGE BASICS

If you can recall singing a song about "a drop of golden sun," you have used *solfège*, a sight-singing system that uses the syllables: *Do-re-mi-fa-sol-la-ti-do.* The pronunciation of *solfège* uses the "pure" vowels discussed earlier in the book.

Using *solfège* is an effective way to practice your exercises, and it will improve your ability to read and learn music quickly. The introductory *solfège* in this book uses the *moveable do* system with no accidentals. Further information about *moveable do* and the *solfège* system can be researched in books, or online. The syllables correspond to the example below.

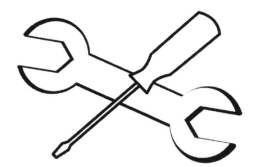

Here is another way to tackle the mysteries of *solfège:*

When singing the exercises in the book, give each *solfège* syllable a number. Singing with syllables and numbers helps to identify the location of the notes in the scale.

DO	1
RE	2
MI	3
FA	4
SOL	5
LA	6
TI	7

12

WORDS, WORDS, WORDS

The International Phonetic Alphabet is a system of letters and symbols that describe sounds. IPA is familiar to us because it is the system used in dictionaries to indicate the pronunciation of words. If you've sung in a language other than your own, you have probably created your own improvised version of "fo-ne-tik lang-widge spel-leengz." Although your individual phonetic system may have worked for the piece you were singing at the time, it's difficult to transfer that work to a new piece of music.

There are numerous advantages to using this standardized system for singing language transcription. Or to be more precise, ðɛr ɑr nʊmərʌs ædvæntədʒəz tu juzɪŋ ðɪs stændərdɑjzd sɪstʌm fɔr sɪŋɪŋ læŋgwədʒ trænskrɪpʃʌn.

- ✓ By reading symbols, you read sounds, not words.

- ✓ By reading symbols, you can look at words transcribed into IPA, and pronounce any language correctly.

- ✓ When you know the symbols for the sounds, you will be able to write text in any language using the International Phonetic Alphabet.

INTERNATIONAL PHONETIC ALPHABET
ɪntərnæʃənʌl fʌnɛtɪk ælfʌbɛt

vawəlz/Vowels

Symbol	Spelling and Position
ɑ	**father**
ɪ	**sit**
i	**see**
ɛ	**bed**
Æ	**Lad**
ʌ	**run, enough**
ɔ	**law, caught, often**
ʊ	**put, wood**
U	**soon, through**
ɚ	**winner, bird, world**

dífθɑŋz/Diphthongs

Symbol	Spelling and Position
ɔɪ	**boy**
ɔu	**no, toe**
ɑu, ɑw	**now**
ju	**pupil**
eɪ	**day, pain**
aɪ	**my, wise**

kansənənts/Consonants

Symbol	Spelling and Position
p	**p**en, s**p**in, ni**p**
b	**b**ut, we**b**
t	**t**wo, s**t**ing, be**t**
d	**d**o, o**dd**
tʃ	**ch**air, na**t**ure, tea**ch**
dʒ	**g**in, **j**oy, e**dg**e
k	**c**at, **qu**een, sti**ck**
g	**g**o, di**g**
f	**f**ool, enou**gh**, lea**f**
v	**v**oice, ha**v**e
θ	**th**ing, tee**th**
ð	**th**is, brea**the**, fa**th**er
s	**s**ee, **c**ity, pa**ss**
z	**z**oo, ro**s**e
ʃ	**s**ure, mo**ti**on, wi**sh**
ʒ	plea**s**ure, bei**g**e
h	**h**am
m	**m**an, hu**m**
n	**n**o, ti**n**
ŋ	si**ng**er, ri**ng**
l	**l**eft, be**ll**
w	**w**e
j	**y**es

English Vowels

Say the words, following the arrows. Notice how the sound "travels" around.

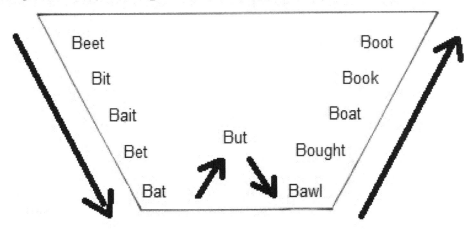

The top of the chart is the front of your mouth.
The bottom of the chart is the back of your mouth.

Some words are easy to say, while others may seem much more complex. For example, consonants and vowels made in the front of the mouth work well together. The word "beet" is fairly easy to say because the sounds (*b, ee, t*) are made close together in the front of the mouth. The word "gong" is also a good combination because of the way these sounds seem to be located "near" each other.

But what if you have to sing about "excellent bagels and tangy sauerkraut from the corner delicatessen"? This bagel-and-sauerkraut song involves a wide range of sounds that use the front and back of the tongue, as well as lips and teeth. Good pronunciation is the result of being able to make all of these sounds easily, without getting "stuck" on any combination of letters. And if there isn't a song about bagels, there should be.

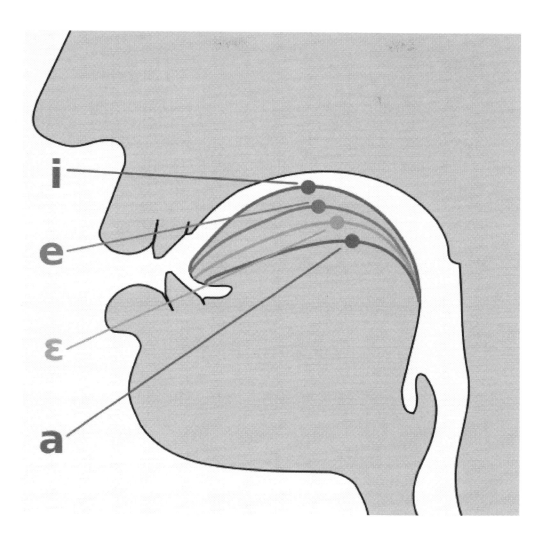

The position of the tongue affects the sound of the vowels, because it changes the shape of the inside of the mouth. The IPA symbols on the left correspond to the vowels in these words: *beet, bait, bet* and *ball.* Say the words, and notice the size of the space between your tongue and the roof of your mouth.

Negotiating the complexities of speech and diction are the same in any language. Learning the International Phonetic Alphabet will give you sound "tools" for every piece of music you will ever sing.

SINGER'S TOOL: LEARNING TO USE SYMBOLS FOR SOUNDS

Here are a few ways to get started with IPA:

- Write IPA symbols for the vowels in your music.

- Add one new consonant symbol at a time.

- Write an English sentence in IPA every day.

- Write the IPA transcription for songs in English.

QUESTIONS

Have you had difficulty remembering how to say the words for music in a language other than your own?

Have you written your own version of phonetic spelling?

Will singing tasks become easier if you have the pronunciation issues under control?

13

MUSIC AND ONLINE RESOURCES

There are many options when it comes to choosing solo vocal music. Beginning and intermediate singers should work with a teacher to choose music in the right range and the correct key. It's also important to choose the appropriate level of difficulty.

I would like to recommend several books that include great music for almost every singer. My list includes the books that have been consistently good studio choices for all of my students. The music I have recommended also provides a good bridge to the standard classical and theatre repertoire for more advanced singers. You may also want to look at the lists for state and regional solo and ensemble festival requirements.

I strongly recommend that all singers learn to play the piano. If lessons are not an option, buy one of the "adult beginner" books designed for piano lessons or piano classes, and learn the basics.

VOCAL MUSIC BOOKS

Folk Songs for Solo Singers, Alfred Music. These books are available in two volumes, and the songs are arranged for high, medium high, and medium low voices with CD accompaniments. The music is always in a comfortable key, the melodies are beautiful and not difficult, and most of the choices in the books are excellent teaching songs.

15 Easy Folksong Arrangements, Hal Leonard Corporation. The books are available for high or low voices, and include the accompaniment CD. These are very nice arrangements, and the beautiful vocal lines are easy for the beginning and intermediate student.

28 Italian Songs and Arias of the 17th and 18th Centuries: Based on the Editions by Alessandro Parisotti, Hal Leonard Corporation. This music is arranged for high, medium high, medium low and low voices, with CD accompaniments. The book contains most of the songs in Schirmer's *Twenty-Four Italian Songs & Arias of the Seventeenth and Eighteenth Centuries,* published a century ago. The Schirmer edition of the Parisotti arrangements is usually among the first books assigned to new students, but the *28 Italian Songs and Arias* book includes translations and IPA transcriptions. The same is true of the *26 Italian Song and Arias: An Authoritative Edition Based on Authentic Sources* from Alfred Music, but the arrangements and ornaments in this edition may not be right for every singer.

The First Book of Solos, Hal Leonard Corporation. These books, edited by Joan Frey Boytim, are an excellent intermediate collection, and there are at least three books for each voice type. CD accompaniments are available. This series includes the main repertoire for many state solo and ensemble festivals.

The Singer's Musical Theatre Anthology - Teen Edition, Hal Leonard Corporation. These books come in soprano, mezzo-soprano/alto, tenor, and baritone/bass keys. The "teen" designation means that they are appropriate for singers in their teens and 20's, or for singers with lighter voices. The songs are in a medium range, and some have been transposed from the original keys. CD accompaniments are available.

Standard Vocal Literature: An Introduction to Repertoire, Hal Leonard Corporation. This collection is for soprano, mezzo, tenor or bass/baritone voices, with a CD supplement that includes accompaniments and diction lessons for the music in languages other than English. The repertoire includes a variety of style periods and composers, as well as an aria and/or a selection from an operetta. These books are excellent for intermediate and advanced students.

The Singer's Musical Theatre Anthology, is a Broadway collection from Hal Leonard Corporation. This is a comprehensive selection of songs for intermediate or advanced singers who are interested in musical theatre. There are at least five volumes of songs for each voice type, plus a set of duet books. All of these books can be ordered with CD accompaniments.

ONLINE RESOURCES

I highly recommend using SmartMusic.com, which is a software system of accompaniments for most of the standard teaching repertoire. An inexpensive student subscription entitles the user to access accompaniments with several features that can be adjusted. Those features include key, tempo, a metronome, and the option to hear the music with or without the melody being played. In addition to being able to access music being studied, a subscription includes access to standard literature for *all* voice types, and standard literature for instrumental music as well. This is a great resource if a student wants to explore music in books for future study.

A note to ensemble teachers: Although the inexpensive yearly subscription access is a great value for any voice or instrumental student taking lessons, this option is a component of a larger music system. The complete system is available to choral and instrumental school music programs, and enables students to practice, record the assignment, and email it to the teacher for assessment. The final result is a classroom full of well-prepared students, which is a teacher's dream come true.

The International Music Score Library Project, imslp.org, is a collection of music in the public domain. This is a vast resource of scores, and contains free, downloadable music in PDF format. The collection contains music for all voice and instrument types.

SINGER'S TOOL: COMPILE YOUR REPERTOIRE LIST

Make a notebook with sections for the different types of music that you have sung. The categories might include:

- Choral music and/or choral solos in English or other languages

- Solo classical or folk music in:

  - English, Italian, German, French, Spanish, Latin

  - Additional languages

- Solo church music

- Popular music

- Solo theatre music

QUESTIONS

Have you sung only one type of music or one language?

Have you ever considered learning a new style of music?

You should learn a variety of styles. Be versatile!

14

VOCALISES
WRITTEN IN THE TREBLE CLEF

VOCALISE #1: LONG TONES AND SLURS

Long, "held" notes are phrases. Think of all the activity that is required for a violinist to play a single, sustained note, because every note has a beginning, a middle and an end. Try moving through every note, rather than waiting for the next pitch.

- ✓ Begin with the lip trill, followed by *thi,* as in "<u>thi</u>ck."

- ✓ Hum on *m*, *n*, or *ng* as in "ki<u>ng</u>."

- ✓ Sing through a straw.

- ✓ Choose a consonant/vowel combination, and sing without changing the vowel as you move from one pitch to another: *ma, ko*, or *sa.*

- ✓ *Solfège*:

  do-re

  re-mi

  mi-fa

  fa-sol

  (Descending)

  sol-fa

  fa-mi

  mi-re

  re-do

VOCALISE #1
LONG TONES AND SLURS

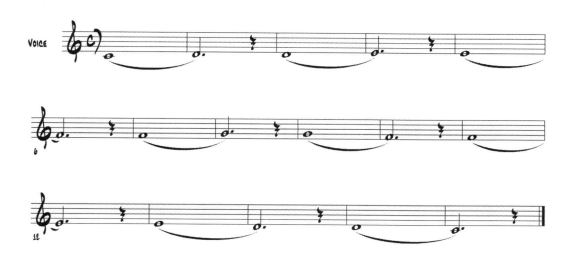

VOCALISE #2: VOWEL PURITY

✓ Begin with the lip trill, followed by *thi,* as in "<u>th</u>ick."

✓ Hum on *m, n*, or *ng* as in "ki<u>ng</u>."

✓ Sing through a straw.

✓ Choose a consonant/vowel combination, and sing without changing the vowel as you move from one pitch to another: *ma, ko,* or *sa.*

✓ *Solfège:*

do-re-do-re-do-re-do

re-mi-re-mi-re-mi-re

mi-fa-mi-fa-mi-fa-mi

fa-sol-fa-sol-fa-sol-fa

(Descending)

mi-fa-mi-fa-mi-fa-mi

re-mi-re-mi-re-mi-re

do-re-do-re-do-re-do

VOCALISE #2

VOWEL PURITY

Voice

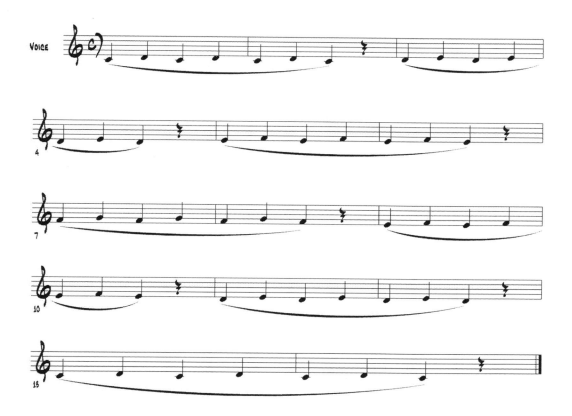

VOCALISE #3: LEGATO

One of your goals should be to make the smooth, connected, unbroken line of sound known as *legato* singing. Even fast-paced music with lots of words will require a good *legato* technique.

- ✓ Begin with the lip trill, followed by *thi,* as in "<u>thi</u>ck."

- ✓ Hum on *m, n,* or *ng* as in "ki<u>ng</u>."

- ✓ Sing through a straw.

- ✓ Use a consonant/vowel combination, and keep the vowel open until you get to the quarter rest: *la, li, mi, ma,* or *si.*

- ✓ *Solfège*:

    do-re-do-re-do

    re-mi-re-mi-re

    mi-fa-mi-fa-mi

    (Descending)

    re-mi-re-mi-re

    do-re-do-re-do

Vocalise #3

Legato

VOCALISE #4: BREATH CONTROL AND LEGATO

Sing each line of music on one vowel/consonant combination, on one breath. Get a full breath at each breath mark.

- ✓ Begin with the lip trill, followed by *thi,* as in "<u>thi</u>ck."

- ✓ Hum on *m, n*, or *ng* as in "ki<u>ng</u>."

- ✓ Sing through a straw.

- ✓ Use a consonant/vowel combination: *no, lu, me,* or *ni.*

- ✓ *Solfège:*

> do-re-do-re-mi-fa-mi-re-do
>
> re-mi-re-mi-fa-sol-fa-mi-re
>
> mi-fa-mi-fa-sol-la-sol-fa-mi

(Descending)

> re-mi-re-mi-fa-sol-fa-mi-re
>
> do-re-do-re-mi-fa-mi-re-do

VOCALISE #4
BREATH CONTROL AND LEGATO

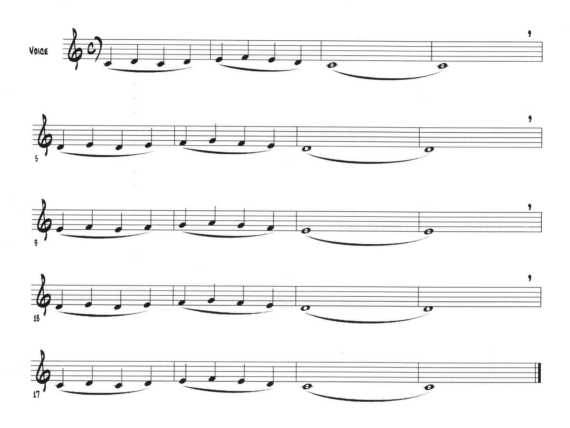

VOCALISE #5: PITCH ACCURACY

This exercise will help you to sing in tune. *Take small, short breaths in each of the rests.* A full breath is not necessary, since you won't be using much when you sing these short notes. It's not necessary to sing loudly. The important thing is to listen.

✓ Begin with the lip trill, followed by *thi,* as in "<u>thi</u>ck."

✓ Sing on *ha, ko, si,* or *lu.*

✓ *Solfège:*

      Measures 1-2 on *do*

      Measures 3-4 on *re*

      Measures 5-6 on *mi*

      Measures 7-8 on *fa*

      Measures 9-10 on *sol*

      Measures 11-12 on *fa*

      Measures 13-14 on *mi*

      Measures 15-16 on *re*

      Measures 17-18 on *do*

VOCALISE #5

PITCH ACCURACY

VOCALISE #6: FLEXIBILITY AND VELOCITY

Singing fast is like driving a car. You need to have complete control over everything you're doing.

- ✓ Begin by singing the music *slowly,* using the lip trill.

- ✓ Sing on *thi,* as in "<u>thi</u>ck."

- ✓ Hum on *m, n*, or *ng* as in "ki<u>ng</u>."

- ✓ Sing through a straw.

- ✓ Sing on *a, e, i, o,* or *u.*

- ✓ Gradually increase the tempo, keeping pitches accurate.

- ✓ *Solfège:*

    do-re-mi-fa-sol-fa-mi-re

    do-re-mi-fa-sol-fa-mi-re-DO

    do-re-mi-fa-sol-la-ti-do-re-do-ti-la-sol-fa-mi-re-DO

    (Repeat)

Vocalise #6

Flexibility and Velocity

VOCALISE #7: DESCENDING AND ASCENDING SCALES

It's important to be able to sing a sustained, connected, *legato* line, and most music requires this technique. Slow scales are challenging, so be sure to use the breath marks.

✓ Begin with the lip trill, followed by *thi,* as in "<u>thi</u>ck."

✓ Hum on *ng* as in "ki<u>ng</u>."

✓ Sing through a straw.

✓ Use a consonant/vowel combination: *la, no,* and *sa.*

✓ *Solfège:*

     do-ti-la-sol-fa-mi-re-do

     do-re-mi-fa-sol-la-ti-do

Vocalise #7

Descending and Ascending Scales

VOCALISE #8 and #9: ARPEGGIO

When the notes in a chord are sung in sequence, one after the other, the result is an *arpeggio*. Singing an *arpeggio* will help you to practice making a sustained, connected, *legato* line while singing intervals. Sing without stopping the sound between notes, and get a full breath at the breath mark.

- ✓ Begin with the lip trill, followed by *thi,* as in "<u>th</u>ick."

- ✓ Hum on *ng* as in "ki<u>ng</u>."

- ✓ Sing through a straw.

- ✓ Use a consonant/vowel combination: *la, no,* and *sa.*

- ✓ *Solfège:*

    #8 do-mi-sol-mi-do

    #9 do-mi-sol-do-sol-mi-do (Repeat)

Vocalise #8

Preparation for Arpeggios

Vocalise #9

One-Octave Arpeggio

VOCALISE #10: ARPEGGIO WITH DESCENDING SCALE

This exercise adds another level of challenge. Sing the *arpeggio* followed by a descending scale, with a change in dynamics. Sing the first four measures *forte* (loud), and the second four measures *piano* (soft). Sing without stopping the sound between notes. Take a full breath at the quarter rest.

- ✓ Begin with the lip trill, followed by *thi,* as in "<u>thi</u>ck."

- ✓ Hum on *ng* as in "ki<u>ng</u>."

- ✓ Sing through a straw.

- ✓ Use a consonant/vowel combination: *la, no,* and *sa.*

- ✓ *Solfège*:

    do-mi-sol-do-ti-la-sol-fa-mi-re-do

VOCALISE #10

ARPEGGIO WITH DESCENDING SCALE

VOCALISE #11: CHANGE OF REGISTER, AND LEGATO LINE

Singing technique is sometimes dependent on whether you are singing in the top, middle, or bottom of your range. Sing a sustained, connected, *legato* line, and take a full breath at the rests.

- ✓ Begin with the lip trill, then hum on *ng* as in "ki<u>ng</u>."

- ✓ Sing through a straw.

- ✓ Use a consonant/vowel combination: *thi* as in *"thick,"* *la, no,* and *sa.*

    Ascending:
    do-re-mi-re-do
    re-mi-fa-mi-re
    mi-fa-sol-fa-mi
    fa-sol-la-sol-fa
    sol-la-ti-la-sol
    la-ti-do-ti-la
    ti-do-re-do-ti, DO

    Descending:
    do-ti-la-ti-do
    ti-la-sol-la-ti
    la-sol-fa-sol-la
    sol-fa-mi-fa-sol
    fa-mi-re-mi-fa
    mi-re-do-re-mi
    re-do-ti-do-re, DO

Vocalise #11

Change of Register and Legato Line

VOCALISE #12: PHRASING AND VOWEL PURITY

This exercise is like a short song, with several notes sung on one vowel/consonant combination as you ascend and descend through your range.

- ✓ Begin with the lip trill, then hum on *ng* as in "ki<u>ng</u>."

- ✓ Sing through a straw.

- ✓ Consonant/vowel combinations: *thi* as in "thick," *la, no,* and *sa.*

- ✓ *Solfège:*

    do-ti-do-re-mi-re-mi-fa-sol

    fa-mi-fa-sol-la-sol-la-ti-do

    do-re-do-ti-la-ti-la-sol-fa

    sol-la-sol-fa-mi-fa-mi-re-do

Vocalise #12

Phrasing and Vowel Purity

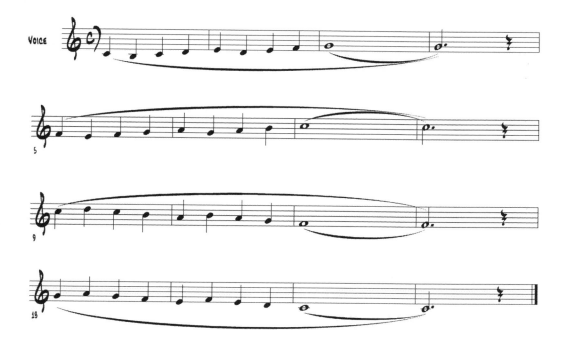

vocalises

connect
scale
arpeggio
phrase
exercise
legato
tone
etude
support
crescendo

15

VOCALISES
WRITTEN IN THE BASS CLEF

VOCALISE #1: LONG TONES AND SLURS

Long, "held" notes are phrases. Think of all the activity that is required for a violinist to play a single, sustained note, because every note has a beginning, a middle and an end. Try moving through every note, rather than waiting for the next pitch.

- ✓ Begin with the lip trill, then sing on *thi*, as in "thick."

- ✓ Hum on *m, n*, or *ng* as in "ki<u>ng</u>."

- ✓ Sing through a straw.

- ✓ Choose a consonant/vowel combination, and sing without changing the vowel as you move from one pitch to another: *ma, ko*, or *sa*.

- ✓ *Solfège:*

    do-re

    re-mi

    mi-fa

    fa-sol

    (Descending)

    sol-fa

    fa-mi

    mi-re

    re-do

VOCALISE #1
LONG TONES AND SLURS

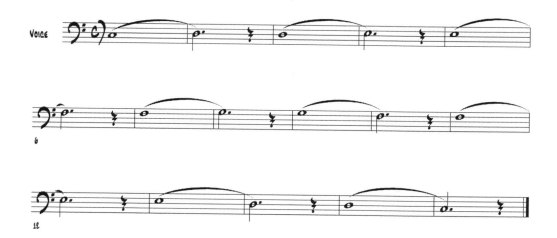

VOCALISE #2: VOWEL PURITY

✓ Begin with the lip trill, then sing on *thi*, as in "thick."

✓ Hum on *m, n,* or *ng* as in "ki<u>ng</u>."

✓ Sing through a straw.

✓ Choose a consonant/vowel combination, and sing without changing the vowel as you move from one pitch to another: *ma, ko*, or *sa*.

✓ *Solfège*:

do-re-do-re-do-re-do

re-mi-re-mi-re-mi-re

mi-fa-mi-fa-mi-fa-mi

fa-sol-fa-sol-fa-sol-fa

(Descending)

mi-fa-mi-fa-mi-fa-mi

re-mi-re-mi-re-mi-re

do-re-do-re-do-re-do

Vocalise #2

Vowel Purity

VOCALISE #3: LEGATO

One of your goals should be to make the smooth, connected, unbroken line of sound known as *legato* singing. Even fast-paced music with lots of words will require a good *legato* technique.

- ✓ Begin with the lip trill, then sing on *thi*, as in "thick."

- ✓ Hum on *m, n,* or *ng* as in "ki<u>ng</u>."

- ✓ Sing through a straw.

- ✓ Choose consonant/vowel combination, and keep the vowel open until you get to the quarter rest: *la, li, mi, ma,* or *si.*

- ✓ *Solfège:*

    do-re-do-re-do

    re-mi-re-mi-re

    mi-fa-mi-fa-mi

    (Descending)

    re-mi-re-mi-re

    do-re-do-re-do

Vocalise #3

Legato

VOCALISE #4: BREATH CONTROL AND LEGATO

Sing each line of music on one consonant/vowel combination, on one breath. Get a full breath at each breath mark.

✓ Begin with the lip trill, then sing on *thi*, as in "thick."

✓ Hum on *m, n*, or *ng* as in "ki<u>ng</u>."

✓ Sing through a straw.

✓ Use a consonant/vowel combination: *no, lu, me,* or *ni.*

✓ *Solfège*:

    do-re-do-re-mi-fa-mi-re-do

    re-mi-re-mi-fa-sol-fa-mi-re

    mi-fa-mi-fa-sol-la-sol-fa-mi

(Descending)

    re-mi-re-mi-fa-sol-fa-mi-re

    do-re-do-re-mi-fa-mi-re-do

Vocalise #4

Breath Control and Legato

VOCALISE #5: PITCH ACCURACY

This exercise will help you to sing in tune. *Take small, short breaths in each of the rests.* A full breath is not necessary, since you won't be using much when you sing these short notes. It's not necessary to sing loudly. The important thing is to listen.

- ✓ Begin with the lip trill, followed by *thi,* as in "<u>thi</u>ck."

- ✓ Sing on *ha, ko, si,* or *lu.*

- ✓ *Solfège*:

    Measures 1-2 on *do*

    Measures 3-4 on *re*

    Measures 5-6 on *mi*

    Measures 7-8 on *fa*

    Measures 9-10 on *sol*

    Measures 11-12 on *fa*

    Measures 13-14 on *mi*

    Measures 15-16 on *re*

    Measures 17-18 on *do*

Vocalise #5

Pitch Accuracy

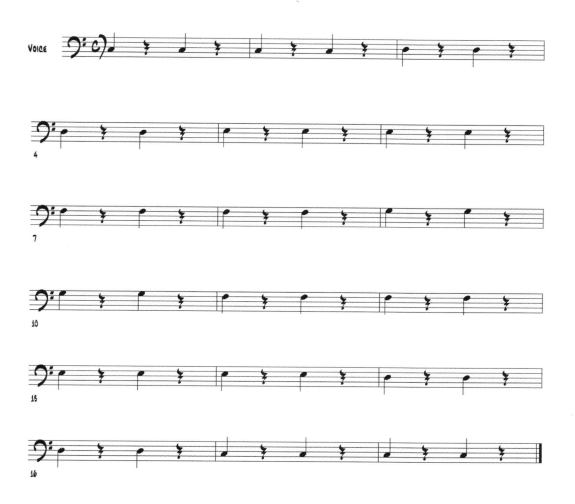

VOCALISE #6: FLEXIBILITY AND VELOCITY

Singing fast is like driving a car. You need to have complete control over everything you're doing.

- ✓ Begin by singing the music *slowly,* using the lip trill.

- ✓ Sing on *thi,* as in "<u>thi</u>ck."

- ✓ Hum on *m, n*, or *ng* as in "ki<u>ng</u>."

- ✓ Sing through a straw.

- ✓ Sing on *a, e, i, o,* or *u.*

- ✓ Gradually increase the tempo, keeping pitches accurate.

- ✓ *Solfège*:

   do-re-mi-fa-sol-fa-mi-re

   do-re-mi-fa-sol-fa-mi-re-DO

   do-re-mi-fa-sol-la-ti-do-re-do-ti-la-sol-fa-mi-re-DO

   (Repeat)

Vocalise #6

Flexibility and Velocity

VOCALISE #7: DESCENDING AND ASCENDING SCALES

It's important to be able to sing a *legato* line, and most music requires this technique. Slow scales are challenging, so be sure to use the breath marks.

- ✓ Begin with the lip trill, then sing on *thi*, as in "thick."

- ✓ Hum on *ng* as in "ki<u>ng</u>."

- ✓ Sing through a straw.

- ✓ Use a consonant/vowel combination: *la, no,* and *sa.*

- ✓ *Solfège*:

    do-ti-la-sol-fa-mi-re-do

    do-re-mi-fa-sol-la-ti-do

VOCALISE #7
DESCENDING AND ASCENDING SCALES

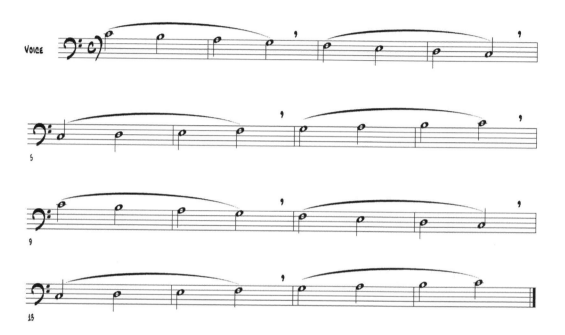

VOCALISE #8 and #9: ARPEGGIO

When the notes in a chord are sung in sequence, one after the other, the result is an *arpeggio*. Singing an *arpeggio* will help you to practice making a sustained, connected, *legato* line while singing intervals. Sing without stopping the sound between notes, and get a full breath at the breath mark.

- ✓ Begin with the lip trill, then sing on *thi*, as in "thick."

- ✓ Hum on *ng* as in "ki<u>ng</u>."

- ✓ Sing through a straw.

- ✓ Use a consonant/vowel combination: *la, no,* and *sa.*

- ✓ *Solfège:*

    #8 do-mi-sol-mi-do

    #9 do-mi-sol-do-sol-mi-do (Repeat)

Vocalise #8
Preparation for Arpeggio

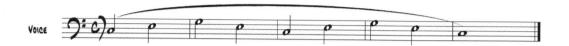

Vocalise #9
One-Octave Arpeggio

VOCALISE #10: ARPEGGIO WITH DESCENDING SCALE

This exercise adds another level of challenge. Sing the *arpeggio* followed by a descending scale, with a change in dynamics. Sing the first four measures *forte* (loud), and the second four measures *piano* (soft). Sing without stopping the sound between notes. Take a full breath at the quarter rest.

- ✓ Begin with the lip trill, then sing on *thi*, as in "thick."

- ✓ Hum on *ng* as in "ki<u>ng</u>."

- ✓ Sing through a straw.

- ✓ Use a consonant/vowel combination: *la, no,* and *sa.*

- ✓ *Solfège*:

     do-mi-sol-do-ti-la-sol-fa-mi-re-do

VOCALISE #10

ARPEGGIO WITH DESCENDING SCALE

VOCALISE #11: CHANGE OF REGISTER, AND LEGATO LINE

Singing technique is sometimes dependent on whether you are singing in the top, middle, or bottom of your range. Sing a sustained, connected, *legato* line, and take a full breath at the rests.

✓ Begin with the lip trill, then hum on *ng* as in "ki<u>ng</u>."

✓ Sing through a straw.

✓ Use a consonant/vowel combination: *thi* as in *"thick,"* *la, no,* and *sa.*

✓ *Solfège:*

> *Ascending:*
> do-re-mi-re-do
> re-mi-fa-mi-re
> mi-fa-sol-fa-mi
> fa-sol-la-sol-fa
> sol-la-ti-la-sol
> la-ti-do-ti-la
> ti-do-re-do-ti, DO
>
> *Descending:*
> do-ti-la-ti-do
> ti-la-sol-la-ti
> la-sol-fa-sol-la
> sol-fa-mi-fa-sol
> fa-mi-re-mi-fa
> mi-re-do-re-mi
> re-do-ti-do-re, DO

VOCALISE #11

CHANGE OF REGISTER AND LEGATO LINE

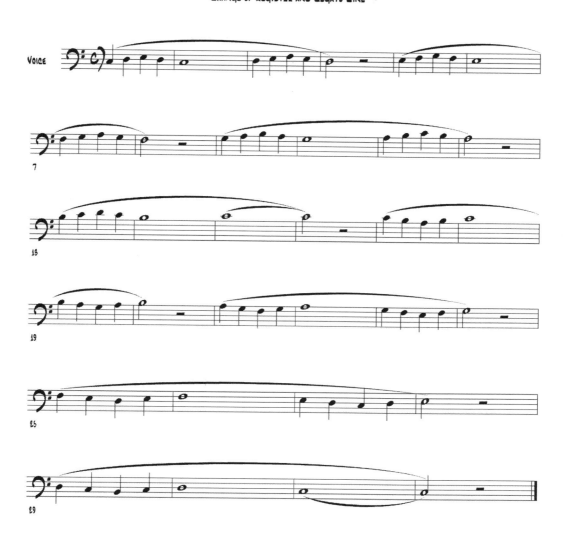

VOCALISE #12: PHRASING AND VOWEL PURITY

This exercise is like a short song, with several notes sung on one consonant/vowel combination as you ascend and descend through your range.

- ✓ Begin with the lip trill, then hum on *ng* as in "ki<u>ng</u>."

- ✓ Sing through a straw.

- ✓ Use a consonant/vowel combination: *thi* as in "thick," *la, no,* and *sa.*

- ✓ *Solfège:*

    do-ti-do-re-mi-re-mi-fa-sol

    fa-mi-fa-sol-la-sol-la-ti-do

    do-re-do-ti-la-ti-la-sol-fa

    sol-la-sol-fa-mi-fa-mi-re-do

VOCALISE #12

PHRASING AND VOWEL PURITY

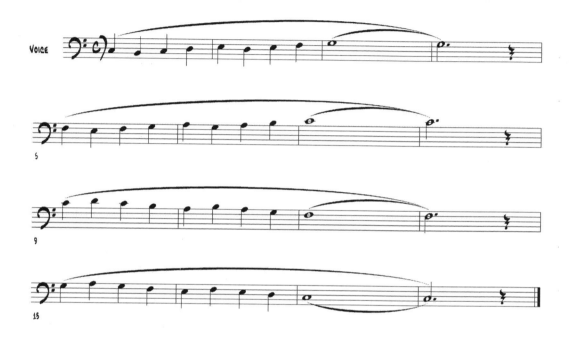

FINAL THOUGHTS

Your mind learns the music, but your body learns to sing. Work to combine the physical skills of singing with the creativity of musical interpretation, and you will accomplish great things.

ABOUT THE AUTHOR

Dr. Vivian Dettbarn-Slaughter teaches voice and piano at the University of Findlay in Ohio, and is a Professor of Sacred Music and Fellow at the Graduate Theological Foundation in Indiana. She has performed in the U.S., Canada and Europe, and is a recipient of the Gupta Award for Teaching Excellence in the Fine Arts at the University of Findlay. Dr. Dettbarn-Slaughter has had a varied career as a teacher, singer, pianist, opera coach, composer, chamber musician, organist, and church music director. She is a member of the National Association of Teachers of Singing, Sigma Alpha Iota International Music Fraternity, Pi Kappa Lambda National Music Honor Society, and the College Music Society. Her music is published by Alliance Publications, Inc.

Made in the USA
San Bernardino, CA
19 February 2020